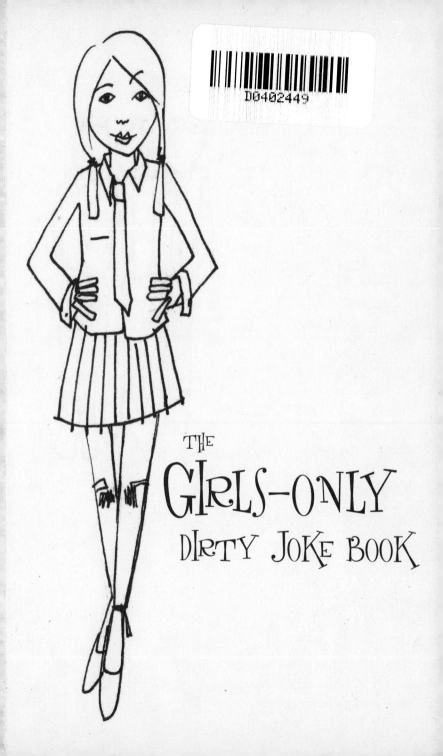

THE

GIRLS-ONLY

DIRTY JOKE BOOK

THE Girls-Only Dirty Joke Book

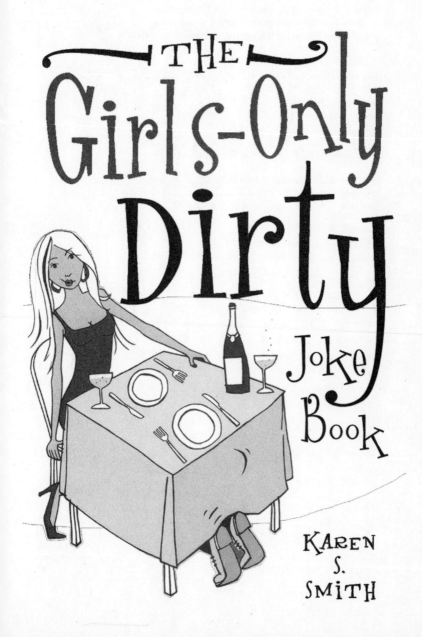

KAREN S. SMITH

Published in the U.S. by
ULYSSES PRESS
P.O. Box 3440
Berkeley, CA 94703
www.ulyssespress.com

First published in the U.K. as *The Best Dirty Girl's Joke Book Ever* in 2005 by Carlton Books Limited

Material for this book has previously appeared under the titles *The Dirty Girl's Joke Book* (Carlton, 2003) and *The Dirty Girl's Joke Book 2* (Carlton, 2005).

ISBN10: 1-56975-648-1
ISBN13: 978-1-56975-648-5
Library of Congress Control Number: 2007907769

Aquisitions Editor: Nick Denton-Brown
Managing Editor: Steven Schwartz
Cover design: Zoë Dissell
Illustrator: Anna Hymas
Editorial and Production:
  Abby Reser, Judith Metzener,
  Elyce Petker

Printed and bound in the United States by Bang Printing

10 9 8 7 6 5 4 3 2 1

THE GIRLS-ONLY
DIRTY JOKE BOOK

Ulysses
Press

CONTENTS

Why do women fake orgasm?

Because men fake foreplay.

What does an atheist miss during orgasm?

Somebody to shout at.

How does a man make a woman scream in bed?

By wiping his dick on the curtains.

A little girl goes to sit on Santa's lap and he asks her what she wants for Christmas. "I want Barbie and Action Man," she says. "Oh," says Santa, "I thought Barbie came with Ken." "No," says the little girl. "Barbie comes with Action Man—she just fakes it with Ken."

Do you know what your asshole does when you have an orgasm?

He shouts, "Hey, what's that buzzing noise coming from the bathroom?"

John says to his girlfriend, "Why don't you shout my name out when you come?"

She answers, "Yeah—like you're ever there when I come!"

How do you know when you've given a good blow job?

He has to pull the bed sheets out of his ass.

A man walks into the bar and sees a sign—"Win Free Drinks for Life"—so he asks the bartender how. "Well," says the bartender, "you have to pass three challenges. First, you have to drink a bottle of tequila. Next, the landlord's pit bull terrier out in the backyard has a toothache—you have to go out and pull that tooth. Finally, the landlord's wife is upstairs and she's never had an orgasm—if you can give one to her, you get free drinks for life." So, the guy thinks he'll give it a try. He takes the bottle of tequila and downs it in one gulp. Then he staggers out into the backyard. There's terrible growling and snarling, and eventually the guy staggers back in, clawed and scratched all over but grinning from ear to ear. "Ok," he says, "that's the first two, now where's that lady with the toothache?"

A woman and a man are riding together in a train. Suddenly, the woman sneezes, starts to writhe around and moan, quivers all over and then goes back to her book. After a few minutes the same thing happens, the sneeze, then the writhing, then the quivering. "Are you all right?" asks the man. "Yes," says the woman, "but I do have an unusual medical condition. Every time I sneeze, I have an automatic orgasm." "Are you taking anything for it?" asks the man. "Yes, pepper," she replies.

A woman goes into a store and asks if they sell batteries. "Yes, we have some in the back room," says the clerk. "Come this way." "If I could come this way," says the woman, "I wouldn't need the batteries."

How do you get a man in your bed, shouting your name and gasping for breath?

Hold a pillow over his face.

Why is a woman like a police car?

They both make a lot of noise to let you know they're coming.

Why is sex like *The Young and The Restless*?

Just when it starts getting interesting, it's all over until tomorrow.

Why don't they let male porn stars work at gas stations?

Because they always pull the nozzle out at the last minute and spray gas all over your windshield.

A woman meets a German in a bar and goes back to his hotel room. He confides that he's a bit kinky, and asks if she would dress up. She says no, so he gets out a big costume, covered in feathers, with a duck's bill and big webbed feet. She thinks this is ok, so she puts it on and they start screwing. He then asks if she would mind putting something else on, and gets out four huge bedsprings. She says ok, so he straps them on her knees and elbows. She gets on all fours and soon they're at it, bouncing away, getting more and more excited.

Finally, he asks her if she'll shout, "Quack! Quack!" As soon as she does this, they both have the most amazing orgasm. "How did you do that?" she asks, as soon as she can speak. "Four-sprung duck technique," he replies.

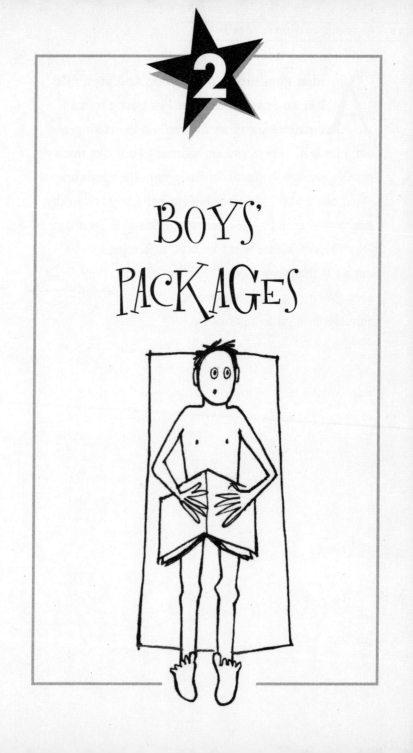

BOYS' PACKAGES

A man goes into a party shop and says, "I'd like to rent a costume; I'm going to a costume party as Adam." So the clerk gets out a fig leaf. "There you are sir, that's $5." "No, that's not big enough," he says, so she gets out a bigger one. "That one's $10." "Still not big enough," he says, so she gets out an even bigger one. "This one's $15," she says. "No, I won't fit into that," he says, so she gets out a hat that says "Exxon." "There," she says. "Wear this, sling it over your shoulder and go as a gas pump."

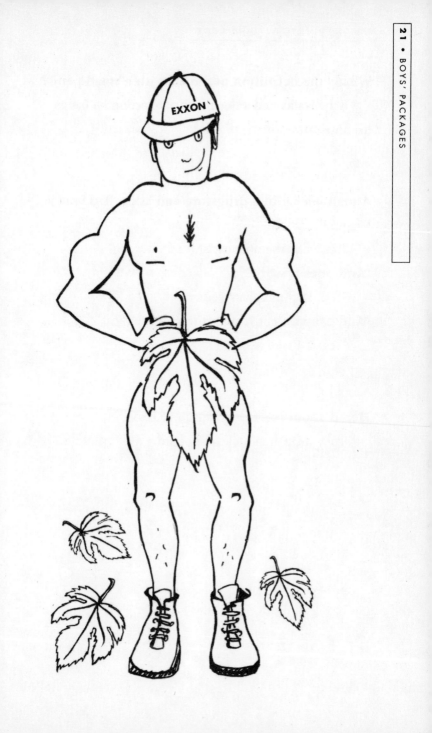

What's the definition of a man with a small penis?

If he walks into a door with an erection he bangs his nose.

A man goes into a drugstore and asks, "Do you sell Viagra?"

"Yes," says the pharmacist.

"And does it work?"

"Yes," says the pharmacist.

"And can you get it over the counter?"

"Yes, if I take two."

Heard about the new Viagra eye drops?

They make him look really hard.

Who's the most popular man on the nude beach?

The one who can carry two cups of coffee and six doughnuts.

Who's the most popular girl on the nude beach?

The one who can eat the sixth doughnut.

How do you get some groovy lovin'?

Use a corduroy condom.

Why did God give men dicks?

So women would have a reason to talk to them.

What's the difference between anal sex and a microwave?

A microwave can't turn your meat brown.

A man goes into a drugstore and asks for something that will keep him hard all night, because he has a hot date with twin sisters, so the pharmacist gives him a tube of stay-hard cream. The next day, he's back in the drugstore, walking a bit strangely and asking for a tube of muscle cream. "You don't want to put muscle cream on your penis," says the pharmacist. "It's not for my penis," says the man. "The twin sisters never showed up so this is for my wrist."

One day Bill noticed that his penis had started growing. He was delighted—and so was his wife—as it rapidly reached six inches, eight inches, then ten inches. By the time it reached 20 inches, however, Bill was finding it difficult to walk, so they went to see a doctor. The doctor examined Bill and said that he could carry out corrective surgery. Bill's wife looked worried at this. "But Doctor," she says, "how long will Bill be in a wheelchair?" "Dear lady," says the doctor, "why should he be in a wheelchair?" "Well, Doctor," she replies, "you are going to lengthen his legs, aren't you?"

Hear about the man with five pricks?

His underwear fit like a glove.

A penis has a sensitive part at one end—called the glans—and an insensitive part at the other—called a man.

A woman calls a male escort agency and asks for the most mind-blowing sex she's ever had. They say they'll send over their best stud, Ramon. A while later, the doorbell rings but when she answers the door, she sees a man with no arms and no legs down on the floor. "I am Ramon," says the man. "You?" says the woman. "How can you give me the most mind-blowing sex I've ever had? You've got no arms and no legs." "Listen, lady," says Ramon, "I rang the doorbell, didn't I?"

A man finds a genie in a bottle, and is offered three wishes. First he asks for a sports car, and poof! There's a shiny red car. Then he asks for a big luxurious house, and poof! There's a huge mansion. Finally he asks to be made irresistible to women. Poof! He turns into a box of chocolates.

Two nuns are sitting on a bench when a streaker runs past. One has a stroke, but the other one can't reach.

How does a dude make up his mind?
He puts mascara on his balls.

How can you spot a blind man on a nude beach?

It's not hard.

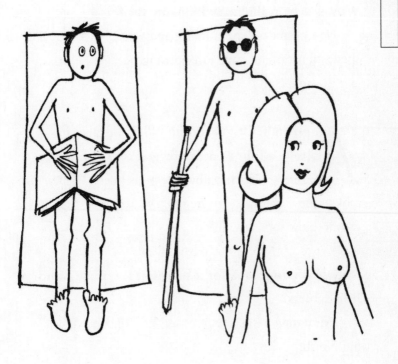

According to women, penises come in three sizes: small, medium and ohmigod.

According to men, there are still three sizes: large, average and size-doesn't-matter.

Why is a man like a Swiss Army knife?

He's meant to have a useful and versatile tool, but he spends most of his time just opening beer.

A girl takes a guy home. When he takes his pants off, he's got the biggest cock she's ever seen—it reaches down past his knees. "You want a blow job?" she says, but he replies, "I'd rather fuck, I can do blow jobs myself."

Why is it dangerous for a man to take Viagra and iron tablets?

Every time he gets an erection he ends up pointing North.

Why does an elephant have four feet?

Six inches would look silly on an elephant.

What's the difference between Niagara and Viagra?

Niagara falls.

What's the definition of stealing Viagra?

A hold-up by hardened criminals.

What do you get if you cross a penis and a potato?

A dictator.

A couple meet in a bar and end up back at his place. "You don't talk much," she says as he's undressing. "No," he says, "I do my talking with this." "Sorry," she says, "I don't do small talk."

3

MEN SAY, WOMEN SAY

Want to come back to my place?

Will both of us fit under the one rock?

Your place or mine?

Both—you go to yours and I'll go to mine.

What's your sign?

No Entry.

If I could see you naked, I'd die happy.

Yeah? If I saw you naked, I'd die laughing.

The word of the day is "legs." Come back to my place and let's spread the word.

Come back when you have enough words for a whole sentence.

I seem to have lost my phone number, can I have yours?

It's ok, I've already got your number.

You know, I like an intelligent woman.

Yeah, I heard opposites attract.

Women can't read maps.

Well, only a man would think an inch equals a mile.

If your tits were a bit firmer, you wouldn't need that bra.

If your cock were a bit firmer, I wouldn't need your brother.

Am I the first man you ever made love to?

You might be—your face looks familiar.

Want to suck it?

Sorry, I choke on small bones.

Haven't I seen you before?

Yes, I'm the receptionist from the VD clinic.

When men say, "Do you have any fantasies?" they mean, "Can we try anal sex/you dressing up as Batgirl/a threesome with your sister?"

When women say, "Do you have any fantasies?" they mean, "I'm so bored that, frankly, I'll try anything."

When men say, "Who else do you like?" they mean, "I like your sister."

When women say, "Who else do you like?" they mean, "You like my sister, don't you?"

4

POINTS TO REMEMBER

Why is a bicycle better than a man?

1. You can ride your bicycle for as long as you like, and it won't get there before you do.

2. A bicycle never complains about having to wear rubber tires.

3. You don't have to shave your legs before you go out on your bicycle.

4. Your parents won't ramble on about how much they liked your old bicycle.

5. Nothing goes soft on a bicycle that a bicycle pump won't fix.

What are the ten worst things about being a penis?

1. Your next door neighbor is an asshole.
2. You can't get excited without wanting to throw up.
3. Every time you get all relaxed, someone takes your sleeping bag away.
4. You're bald all your life but with really hairy feet.
5. You've always got two nuts hanging around you.
6. Your home is underwear.
7. In cold weather you shrink.
8. You've only got one eye.
9. Every time your owner remembers you're there, he tries to strangle you.
10. Women would rather see you stiff.

Ten things not to say to a naked man:

1. Is it really that size, or are you standing far away?
2. Oh, are we skipping straight to the cigarette?
3. Very funny, now put the real one back on.
4. I hope your tongue is bigger than that.
5. Oh well, no hard feelings.
6. And what does it want to be when it grows up?
7. You know, maybe we should go fishing instead?
8. And your shoes were so huge.
9. Still, no danger of a gag reflex tonight.
10. Never mind, if we plant it maybe a great oak will grow.

If men had a vagina for a day, they would:

1. Wonder what the little pink button next to it does.

2. Lie in bed all morning with a hand mirror.

3. Get up and go shopping for cucumbers.

4. Go to church and pray for breasts as well.

5. Secretly worry about whether it was bigger than everybody else's.

6. Lie in bed all afternoon with a home video camera.

7. Finally find that damn g-spot that all the fuss is about.

8. Get picked up in a bar without even trying.

9. Have an orgasm—then have another one without needing a nap first.

10. Repeat number 9.

If women had a penis for a day, they would:

1. Measure it to see whether that really is six inches.
2. Pee standing up, without even trying to hit the toilet.
3. Get a blow job.
4. Fall asleep without saying thanks.
5. Wake up.
6. Repeat number 3.
7. Repeat number 3.
8. Repeat number 3.
9. Repeat number 3.
10. Repeat number 3.

Why are dogs better than men?

1. If a dog wants to go out, it will let you know.
2. A dog will express affection in public.
3. A dog will play ball without telling you how to throw overarm.
4. You can train a dog to understand what "no" means.
5. If a dog wants its balls licked, it will do it for itself.
6. After six months, a dog will still look excited to see you.

7. Just because you've had some fun with a dog, it doesn't think it can sleep on your bed.

8. Dogs feel guilt.

9. Dogs are grateful when you stroke them.

10. When your dog gets old, you can just get a younger dog.

Cars are better than sex because:

1. You get a manual with your car—"Sudden failure of big end? Wait for excess alcohol to drain out of system. Turnover rate too rapid? Clean all points of contact with a wire brush."

2. Your car is insured against accidental injury to a third party—"Dear Madam, with regards to your claim, our client says that your husband went straight into her rear while she was stationary and waiting to enter an intersection—therefore she cannot accept any responsibility."

3. If your escort has an accident, they will lend you a replacement while they fix it—the replacement is usually faster, younger and shinier.

4. A car doesn't need emotional maintenance, just a drop of oil every month or so.

5

STAYING TOGETHER

A newlywed couple is getting undressed for the first time, and the husband says, "Darling, your body is so beautiful—let me get my camera and take a picture." "Why?" asks his wife. "So that I can keep it with me always and remember how beautiful you are," he says. Then he takes his clothes off and she says, "Darling, I must also take a photograph of you." "Why?" asks her husband. "So I can get it enlarged," she replies.

What do you call a woman without an asshole?

Divorced.

Why are men like fine wine?

It takes a lot of trampling and keeping them in the dark before they mature into something you'd want to have dinner with.

What do you do if your boyfriend starts smoking?

Slow down.

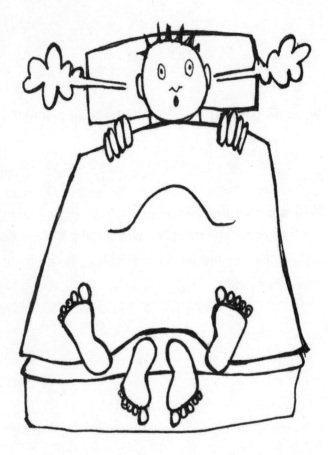

Name the disease that paralyzes women below the waist?

Marriage.

If he can't get it up, you can go down, but if he can't get it in, get out.

A married couple answers the door to find a bald gnome holding a mirror. "This is a magic mirror," says the bald gnome. He hangs it on the front door and offers to demonstrate it. Rubbing his head, the gnome says, "Mirror, mirror, on the door, make me hairy as before." With a flash, the gnome has a full head of hair. Impressed, the couple buy the mirror, take it into the bedroom and hang it on the bedroom door. First the woman goes up to the mirror, rubs her breasts and says, "Mirror, mirror, on the door, make my breasts a 44." There's a flash, and instantly she has 44-inch breasts. The husband is terribly excited—he rushes over to the mirror, rubbing his cock furiously, and shouts, "Mirror, mirror, on the door, make my penis touch the floor." There's a huge flash, and instantly his legs disappear.

How do married couples use Vaseline to help with their sex lives?

They put it on the bedroom doorknob to keep the kids out.

Oral sex can make your day, but anal sex can make your hole weak.

What's the difference between embarrassment, worry and panic?

Embarrassment is the first time a man can't get it up for the second time.

Worry is the first time he can't get it up for the first time.

Panic is the second time he can't get it up for the first time.

What's the difference between men and fine wine?

You don't have to roll a man around in your mouth to get the most enjoyment out of him.

In Heaven, the lovers are French, the comedians are American and the engineers are German.

In Hell, the comedians are German, the engineers are French and the lovers are American.

6

SLUTTY BITCH STORIES

Three women are in the vet's waiting room with their dogs. "What a lovely labrador," says one. "What are you bringing him in for?" "He is lovely," says the owner, "But he's a terrible chewer. He's chewed the furniture and my husband's shoes, but the final straw was when he chewed up my husband's golfclubs and left nothing but a pile of sawdust. So my husband said that either the dog goes, or he goes." "So you're having him put to sleep?" "I'm afraid so," says the owner.

The second dog is a collie. "What a lovely collie, what are you bringing him in for?" "He is lovely but he's a terrible chaser. He chases cars, he chases bicycles, he even chases the postman. The final straw came when he chased my husband's mother down the driveway and out of the gate. So my husband said that either the dog goes, or he goes." "So you're having him put to sleep?" "Yes, I'm afraid so."

So they turn to the third dog. "What a lovely Great Dane." "He is lovely, but he's a terrible humper. He'll hump anything—the sofa, the neighbor's dog, the pastor's leg. The final straw was when I was getting out of the shower. I bent over to pick up the soap and in no time he was on top of me, humping away. It took my husband ten minutes to pull him off, and that was it—my husband said that either that dog goes, or I go." "So you're having him put to sleep?" "Oh no, I've just brought him in to have his claws trimmed."

A Hell's Angel drops his motorbike off to be fixed, and is walking home. On the way he remembers that he's supposed to be picking up some things at the hardware store for the Hell's Angel Clubhouse. "Ah, yes," says the shopkeeper, "Here you are," and he gets out a bucket, an anvil, a goat, an ax and a black rooster. "How am I supposed to carry all this without my bike?" says the Hell's Angel. "Well," says the shopkeeper, "You could put the rooster under one arm, the anvil under the other arm, put the ax in the bucket and hold it in one hand, then lead the goat with the other hand." So the Hell's Angel does as the shopkeeper suggests and starts walking back to the clubhouse. A few yards down the road, he's stopped by a little old lady. "Excuse me, young man," she says. "Can you tell me the way to the chapel?" "It's right next to our clubhouse," says the Hell's Angel. "Come with me and I'll show you the way. It's just down this alley." The old lady looks at him very suspiciously. "Young man," she says, "you are a tall, hairy, muscular man and I am a helpless old woman. How do I know you won't get me half way down that alley, push me roughly against the wall, pull down my panties and take me roughly 'til your wicked desires are satiated?" "Madam," he replies, "I have a bucket in one hand with an ax in it, a goat on a string in the other hand, an anvil under one arm and a rooster under the other arm, how could I possibly push you roughly against any wall?" So the old lady says, "Put the rooster down, put the bucket over the rooster and the anvil on top of the bucket, lay the ax on the ground and I'll hold on to the goat."

A man walks into a bar with a frog. He puts the frog on the bar and orders a pint and a packet of peanuts. Then he says, "Billy—catch!" and throws the peanuts to the frog, one at a time, who catches them in its mouth. "Wow," says the barmaid, "a performing frog!" "Yes," says the man. "This frog can do all sorts of tricks. It catches peanuts, it fetches a stick— and it gives the best cunnilingus in the world." The barmaid can't believe her ears, so the man says if she doesn't believe him, she can try it for herself. At closing time, the barmaid takes the man and the frog upstairs and lies naked on the bed.

The man puts the frog gently down between her legs but the frog does nothing. "Billy—cunnilingus!" says the man. Still the frog does nothing. "Oh, for heavens sake Billy," says the man. "How many times do I have to show you?"

A guy gets a new sports car and takes his girlfriend out for a spin. She keeps telling him to go faster and faster, but at around 100 miles an hour he gets a bit scared. "If I take off my top, will you do 120?" He says yes, so she takes off her top and he does 120. "If I take off all my clothes, will you do 150?" she asks. He says yes, so she takes off all her clothes, and he does 150. "If I give you a blow job, will you do 200?" He says yes, so she starts giving him a blow job and he puts his foot all the way down. Before they know it, they've run off the road, she's been thrown from the car and he's trapped under it with only one foot sticking out. She tries to pull him out, but his shoe just comes off. "Go and get help!" he shouts. "I can't, I'm naked and all my clothes are trapped under the car," she says. But there's nothing else to be done, so she covers her privates with his shoe, runs to the nearest house and bangs on the door. An old farmer opens the door and she starts shouting, "Please, you've got to help me, my boyfriend's stuck. Can you help me pull him out?" The old farmer looks slowly down at the shoe and says, "Nope, I reckon he's too far in for that."

A ventriloquist is out on a country walk, and sees a farmer leaning on a gate. "Afternoon," says the ventriloquist. "Afternoon," says the farmer. Then the ventriloquist turns to the farmer's dog. "Afternoon," he says to the dog, and "Afternoon," comes the dog's reply. The farmer looks amazed, but he doesn't say anything. "This your master?" asks the ventriloquist. "Yep," says the dog. "And how does he look after you?" "Oh, pretty well," says the dog. "He feeds me, lets me sleep in the kitchen and pats me now and then." The farmer looks amazed, but he says nothing. "I see you've got a horse," says the ventriloquist. "Mind if I talk to him?" "Go ahead," says the farmer. "Afternoon," says the ventriloquist. "Afternoon," the horse replies. The farmer is looking more and more surprised, but still he says nothing. "How does the farmer look after you?" asks the ventriloquist. "Oh, pretty well," says the horse. "He feeds me, I have my own stable, and he takes me out for a trot every day." Then the ventriloquist looks into the field behind the farmer and says, "I see you have some sheep…" "Oh," says the farmer, "those sheep are liars! Those sheep are liars!"

Four nuns die and go to Heaven. At the Pearly Gates, Saint Peter stops them. "Before you enter Heaven, you must be completely pure," he says. "Sister Mary, have you ever had the slightest contact with a man's penis?" "I must confess that I have," says Sister Mary, "I once saw a man's penis." "Wash your eyes out with this holy water and pass into Heaven," says Saint Peter. "Now, Sister Martha, have you ever had the slightest contact with a man's penis?" "I must confess that I have," says Sister Martha, "I once stroked a man's penis with my hand." "Wash your hand in this holy water and pass into Heaven" says Saint Peter. But before he can get any further, the other two nuns have started pushing and shoving. "Sisters!" says Saint Peter sternly, "There is room for all in the Kingdom of God—what is the meaning of this unseemly scuffling?" "If I'm going to have to gargle with that holy water," says the fourth nun, "I want to get to it before Sister Catherine sticks her fat ass in it."

A man goes into a pharmacy and asks to speak to a male pharmacist, since he has an embarrassing problem. "I'm sorry," says the female pharmacist. "My sister and I run this shop, you'll have to speak to one of us about it." Well, the man's very embarrassed, but he tells her that he's had a permanent hard-on for the last year and whatever he does, he can't get rid of it for more than ten minutes. "Can you give me anything for it?" The pharmacist says she needs to consult her sister, and two minutes later comes back and says, "The best we can manage is $50,000 a year and a third share of the shop."

Tonto and the Lone Ranger are riding through the desert, when Tonto pulls on the reins of his horse and dismounts. He kneels down and presses his ear to the ground, while the Lone Ranger waits in silence. Finally Tonto raises his head, nods wisely and speaks. "Buffalo come."

"Amazing!" says the Lone Ranger. "Your Indian lore never fails to impress me. Tell me, Tonto, how can you tell?" Tonto speaks again, "Ear sticky."

Two men see a dog licking his own balls. "I wish I could do that," says the first man, "You can," says the second man, "if you give him a biscuit first."

A nun is sitting in the bath when there's a knock on the door. "Who is it?" she says. "It's the blind man," comes the reply. So she thinks it will be all right, since he won't see her naked and tells him to come in. The man comes in and says, "Holy cow, a naked nun! Now, where do you want this venetian blind?"

A woman goes to buy a parrot, and the shopkeeper says, "We've got one for $100, one for $200 and one for $15." "Why is that one so cheap?" asks the woman. "Well, it used to live in a brothel, so it has a pretty dirty mouth." The woman says she

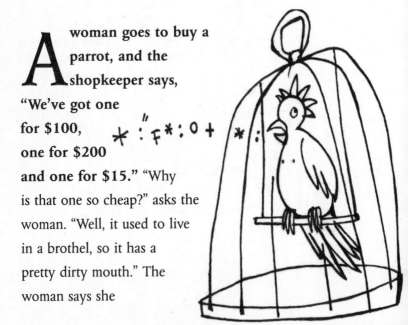

doesn't mind, so she pays her $15 and takes the parrot home. As soon as she takes the cover off the cage, the parrot says, "Fuck me, a new brothel!" Then he looks at the woman and says, "Fuck me, a new Madam." "I am not a Madam, and this is not a brothel," says the woman, but she thinks it's pretty funny. Later on, her two teenage daughters come in. "Fuck me," says the parrot, "New prostitutes!" "We are not prostitutes," say the daughters, but they think it's pretty funny too. "Wait 'til Dad comes in and hears this parrot, he'll lose it." So they put the parrot in the hall, the door opens and Dad comes in. Dad looks at the parrot, and the parrot looks at him, then the parrot says, "Fuck me, Dave, haven't seen you for weeks."

7

eVery QuestIon HAS An AnsWer

What's the difference between a fake dollar and a skinny man?

One's a phoney buck, the other's a bony fuck.

Why do men whistle on the toilet?

It helps them remember which end to wipe.

What's the difference between a 69 and driving in fog?

When you're driving in fog, you can't see the asshole in front of you.

Why is sex like a bungee jump?

It's over in no time, and if the rubber breaks, you're in trouble.

Why did the pervert cross the road?

He couldn't get his dick out of the chicken.

What's the difference between a man and a jellybean?

Jellybeans come in different colors.

Why do cowgirls have bow legs?

Because cowboys never take their hats off, even when they're eating.

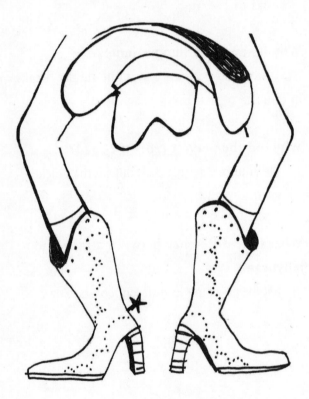

What's the difference between a man and a condom?

Condoms aren't thick and insensitive these days.

Why is a hangover better than a man?

A hangover is usually gone by lunchtime.

Why are men like cowpies?

The older they get, the easier they are to pick up.

What's the best thing about a nudist wedding?

It's easy to spot the Best Man.

What do you call a beautiful woman on the arm of an ugly man?

A tattoo.

Why is a woman like a TV remote control?

Because a man will just sit there pushing buttons randomly until something happens.

Why is a man like a dining room table?

They both have an extra part that extends for entertaining.

Why do bald men have holes in their pockets?

So they can run their fingers through their hair.

What is warm and soft when a man comes home drunk at night and hard and stiff when he wakes up in the morning?

The pile of puke at the bottom of the stairs.

Why is cheap beer like having sex in a canoe?

They're both fucking close to water.

What do you do to make five pounds of fat look sexy?

Put them in a push-up bra.

What's the definition of a slut?

A woman with the sexual morals of a man.

Why is car insurance cheaper for women?

Because women don't get blow jobs while they're driving.

Why is a guy like a computer?

You don't realize how much either of them means to you until they go down on you.

What's the best thing about sex with a clown?

You know what they say about men with big feet.

And the worst thing?

Infidelity: you'll catch him having sex with the contortionist behind her back.

What's the best thing about sex with a taxi driver?

He's never in a hurry to get from A to B. In fact, he'll usually take as long as he can.

And the worst thing?

You can never tell when he's going to pull out.

What's the best thing about sex with a bank teller?

The bigger the deposit and the longer you leave it in, the more interest you get.

And the worst thing?

He's not so into withdrawals.

What's the best thing about sex with a motorcycle messenger?

He's dressed completely in leather and he's really, really dirty.

And the worst thing?

He's always slipping into narrow spaces where he's not supposed to go.

What's the definition of an ugly man?

Even his computer won't go down on him.

What's the difference between an egg and a jerk?

You can beat an egg.

PUSSY POWER

What did the banana say to the vibrator?

I don't know why you're trembling—I'm the one she's going to eat!

How do you know who gives the best cunnilingus?

Word of mouth.

What's the difference between a genealogist and a gynecologist?

One looks up your family tree and the other just looks up your bush.

What's the difference between a pussy and a grill?

Nobody minds if you stab their sausage with a fork before you put it in your grill.

What's the difference between pussy and apple pie?

Any man will eat his mother's apple pie.

How does a policewoman part her hair?

(bending knees) "Hello, hello, hello…"

Why don't women blink during foreplay?

No time.

Why don't the maxi pads talk to the tampons?

Because they're stuck up cunts.

Why do women have two pairs of lips?

One to talk to a man and one to shut him up.

Why do women rub their eyes in the morning?

Because they don't have balls.

What's white, eight inches long, takes two batteries, gives complete satisfaction in three minutes and once you've tried it you'll never go back to the manual method?

An electric toothbrush.

What do you call a man with a twelve-inch tongue who can hold his breath for ten minutes?

Nothing, just keep hold of his ears.

What's the definition of a man with a long tongue?

When he sticks it out for the doctor, the nurse goes, "Aaaah!"

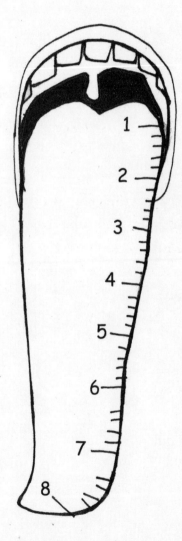

9

WHO SAYS BLONDES ARE STUPID?

Why do blondes have more fun?

They're more easily impressed.

Why did the blonde have sex with the lights on?

She left the car door open.

Why do a blonde's brain cells die?

They're lonely.

Why do blondes make bad dairy farmers?

They can't keep two calves together.

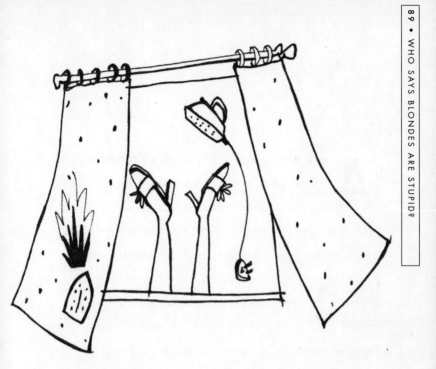

Heard about the blonde girl who decided to iron the curtains?

She fell out of the window.

Why don't blondes look out the window in the morning?

They'd have nothing to do in the afternoon.

A guy walks into a bar with a crocodile. He sits on a bar stool, gets out a big stick and hits the crocodile once around the head. The crocodile opens its mouth wide, the man unzips his fly, gets his cock out and puts it in the crocodile's mouth. The man then hits the crocodile again with the stick and it gently closes its mouth, as the whole bar holds its breath. Finally, the man gives the crocodile another sharp tap with the stick. It opens its mouth again and he takes his cock out and puts it back in his pants. "So," he says, "if anyone else wants to try that, I'll give them a hundred dollars." Silence. Everyone stares at the crocodile.

"Come on," says the man, "a hundred dollars for anyone who'll do it." Then a blonde girl pipes up from the back, "I'll give it a try, but please don't hit me so hard with that stick."

Two blondes are planning a bank robbery. One of them stays in the car with the engine running and the other one pulls on a balaclava. "Now," says the getaway driver, "you've got the gun?" "Yes." "You've got the rope?" "Yes." "And you've got the dynamite." "Yes." "Go for it!" So the blonde runs into the bank. She's been gone a long time and no explosion. Then she's been gone a very long time and still no explosion. The getaway driver is about to give up and drive off when the blonde runs out of the bank—no money, balaclava half off, pursued by a security guard with his trousers around his ankles—and jumps in the car. As they speed off, the getaway driver says, "I tell you every time— you're supposed to tie up the guard and blow the safe."

Two blonde girls walk into a building. You'd think at least one of them would have seen it.

A blonde, a brunette and a redhead get into an elevator, and notice a white sticky patch on the wall. "That's funny," says the brunette. "That looks like cum." The redhead sniffs the air and says, "Yep, and it smells like cum." The blonde puts her finger in the sticky patch, licks her finger and says, "Well, it's nobody from our office."

Why is a blonde girl like a beer bottle?

They've both got nothing but air from the neck up.

What's the difference between a blonde and a road sign?

Road signs sometimes say "Stop."

What does a blonde do with her asshole in the morning?

Give him his packed lunch and send him to work.

Why did the blonde swap her car for a convertible?

She wanted the extra legroom.

Three blond men find an old bottle. When they open it, a genie pops out and offers them a wish each. "Awesome!" says the first blond. "I'd like you to make me more intellig… intellig… not so stupid." Poof! There's a puff of smoke and the guy has red hair. So the second blond guy says, "I'd like to be even more intellig… intellig… even less stupid than he is." Poof! Another puff of smoke, and the second guy has brown hair. So the third blond says, "I'd like to be even more intellig… intellig… even less stupid than both my friends." Poof! There's a third puff of smoke and when it clears, he's still blond, but now he's a woman.

A blonde girl has a baby, and the family all come to visit. They ask to see the baby, but she says, "Not yet, it's asleep." They wait a while and then they ask again. "Not yet, it's asleep," comes the answer. Finally it's getting late and they have to leave, so they ask once more to see the baby. "Not yet, it's asleep. You have to wait until it cries," comes the answer. "Why do we have to wait until it cries?" they ask. "Because I forgot where I put it down."

What's the hardest thing to hit a blonde girl with?
A new idea.

A blonde is walking down the street with her blouse unbuttoned and her right breast hanging out. A policeman stops her and says, "Madam—are you aware that I could arrest you for indecent exposure. You can't walk along the street with your breast hanging out." The blonde looks down and says, "Oh goodness—I left the baby on the bus again!"

95 • WHO SAYS BLONDES ARE STUPID?

What's the difference between a clever blonde and a dumb blonde?

The clever blondes have dark roots showing.

What's the difference between a blonde girl and a light bulb?

The light bulb is brighter, but the blonde is easier to turn on.

How do you know when you've got a blonde gardener?

The bushes are slightly darker than the rest of the garden.

A blonde is crossing the road when a car hits her. The driver rushes over to see if she's ok. "My eyes, my eyes," she shouts. "Everything's blurry! I'm going blind!" The driver's worried that he might have really injured her, so he says, "How many fingers have I got up?" "Oh no!" she cries. "Don't say I'm paralyzed from the waist down as well!"

A blonde girl is staying in an expensive hotel and decides she'll try a milk bath, so she calls down to reception and asks them to send up 30 pints of milk to fill up the bath. "Pasteurized?" asks the receptionist. "No, just up to my tits," replies the blonde.

Why do blondes wear panties?

To keep their ankles warm.

What does a blonde girl do for foreplay?

Warm her ankles.

What two things in the air can get a blonde girl pregnant?

Her legs.

What's the difference between a blonde girl and the Million Man March?

Only a million men did the march.

What's the difference between a blonde girl and the Titanic?

They know how many men went down on the Titanic.

What's the difference between a blonde and a politician?

A blonde only screws one person at a time.

Blonde girl goes to the doctor and says, "I hurt all over." She presses her finger into her knee, "That hurts." Then she presses her finger into her stomach, "That hurts," and then she presses her finger into her forehead, "Even that hurts. What is it, doctor?" The doctor replies, "You have a broken finger."

Do blondes really have more fun?

Yes, they just can't remember who with.

How many blondes does it take to change a light bulb?

Just one—and a dozen men to look up her skirt while she does it.

Heard about the other blonde chef who could only cook chicken in apple cider sauce?

She couldn't have a cock in her hand without wanting it in cider.

Why did the blonde girl have sunglasses inside her panties?

The weather forecast said there would be sunny periods.

Why did the blonde girl have lipstick on her steering wheel?

She was trying to blow her horn.

Why do men call blondes "dolls"?

Because when you lay them on their backs, their eyes close.

Why do men like blonde girl jokes?

Because they can understand them.

10

FIRST IMPRESSIONS

Wanna have a quickie?

Can you do any other kind?

I'm an expert in mouth-to-mouth resuscitation—want a demonstration?

I'd have to be completely dead before I'd let you get that close.

I can give you supersex.

I'll take the soup, thanks.

Do you like it doggy style?

Yes—you can beg all you like, and I'll roll over and play dead.

What's your sign?

Private Property.

Can I give you my number?

Yes, I'll call you when my dog's in heat.

I'd like to get in your pants.

I already have one asshole in my pants, thanks.

Hey, angel, pull up a cloud and sit down.

Sorry, angels can only talk to people who are dead—dead from the neck up doesn't qualify.

Your place or mine?

Well... I'm running out of places to hide the bodies at mine...

I have a telepathic watch. It tells me you're not wearing any underwear.

I'm afraid I am wearing underwear.

Damn, the thing's an hour fast again.

What's a nice girl like you doing in a place like this?

If I were a nice girl, I wouldn't be in a place like this.

That dress is very becoming on you.

But the question is—would I be coming on you?

Are you an optical spanner? Because every time you look at me I feel my nuts tighten.

Lucky you've got nuts because you're not getting a screw.

Nice legs—what time do they open?

Sorry, it's full, members only.

If I bought you some underwear, would there be anything in it for me?

Yes, the knowledge that you'd made my boyfriend very happy.

If we are what we eat, I could be you by tomorrow morning.

No, by tomorrow morning you'll just be 18 pints of beer.

Do you come here often?

No, it's just the way I laugh.

Would you like another drink?

No, if one doesn't make you look attractive, I don't think two will do the trick.

I'm a magician—want to see my wand?

Can it make you disappear?

A 13-year-old boy goes into a bar and says to the barmaid, **"Get me a double Scotch on the rocks."** "What do you want to do," asks the barmaid, "get me in trouble?" "Maybe later," says the kid, "but I'll start with the Scotch."

Where have you been all my life?

Where I'll be the rest of your life—in your wildest dreams.

I could make you the happiest woman on earth.

You're leaving so soon?

Haven't I seen you somewhere before?

Yes, that's why I stopped going there.

I wish you were a door—I could bang you all day.

I doubt it; you don't have a key that would fit my lock.

You've got lovely eyes...

Yes, they saw you coming.

Why is a beautiful girl like you still single?

Just lucky, I guess.

We could be having wild sex by midnight tonight.

We probably will be—but not with each other.

Where have you been all my life?

Outside your window, in the bushes, with binoculars.

Is that a run in your stocking or a stairway to heaven?

You have to be good to go to heaven. Really good.

Can I buy you a drink?

Can I just have the money?

11

HOW DO YOU KNOW WHEN?

How do you know when you're in bed with a policeman?

He asks you to blow into his breathalyzer.

How do you know when you're in bed with a fireman?

He comes when you're hot and leaves you soaking wet.

How do you know when you're in bed with a mathematician?

He divides your legs and then he subtracts his root so you don't multiply.

How do you know when you're in bed with a postman?

He doesn't come when he's supposed to, and half the time it's in the wrong slot.

How do you know when you're in bed with an explorer?

He goes deeper into the bush than any man has ever been.

How do you know when you're in bed with an astronaut?

The equipment is huge, but there's no atmosphere.

How do you know when you're in bed with a takeaway chef?

You ask for 69 and he gives you egg-fried rice.

How do you know when you're in bed with an archaeologist?

They'll date anything.

How do you know when you're in bed with a blacksmith?

He hammers away for hours and then he makes a bolt for the door.

How do you know when you've found Mr. Right?

His first name is "Always."

How can you tell when your husband is dead?

The sex is the same, but the smell of farts has vanished.

How can you tell when a woman is frigid?

When she opens her legs a light comes on.

Why did God create alcohol?

So ugly people could get laid.

How can you tell when a man is well-hung?

His face is blue and he's stopped struggling.

How do you know when you're getting old?

You can sleep with someone half your age without breaking any laws.

How do you know when you're using food as a substitute for sex?

You can't even get into your own pants.

How do you know when a man is sexually aroused?

He has a pulse.

How do you know when a hitchhiker is a witch?

When she strokes the driver's leg he turns into a rest stop.

How do you get a man to always leave the toilet seat down?

Cut off his penis.

What is 69 + 69?

Dinner for four.

Why do men get married?

So they can stop holding their stomachs in.

Why are men's brains bigger than women's brains?

So they can think of excuses.

How do you spot the sex-crazed whale?

She's the one who'll suck the end off a submarine and swallow the seamen.

Why do they name hurricanes after women?

Because they're wild, wet and noisy when they come—and when they go you lose your house and your car.

Why are breasts like toy trains?

They're both intended for children but usually get played with by men.

What food diminishes your sex drive by 75%?

Wedding cake.

Why does only one sperm out of millions get to the egg?

Because they refuse to stop and ask for directions.

Why does a penis have a big head on the end?

To stop the man's hand from sliding off and hitting him in the eye.

Why is Viagra like an amusement park?

They both make you wait two hours for a three-minute ride.

Why is sex like playing bridge?

If you don't have a good partner, you'd better have a good hand.

Why do female spiders bite the heads off their mates after sex?

It's the only way to stop them from snoring.

Why is a dildo like a soy bean?

They're both a substitute for meat.

Why are men like tights?

They never quite fit between the legs, and they usually run after one night out.

Why can't Miss Piggy count to 70?

Because when she gets to 69 she has a frog in her throat.

Why do women prefer a circumcised penis?

Because anything with 10% off is always attractive.

When did Pinocchio realize he was made of wood?

When his hand caught fire.

If mothers have Mother's Day and fathers have Father's Day, what do bachelors have?

Palm Sunday.

What's a shotgun wedding?

It's a wife-or-death situation.

Why doesn't Popeye's favorite tool go rusty?

He puts it in Olive Oil.

How do you know which girl in a Catholic school is the head girl?

She's the one with the dirty knees.

How do you get a man to really listen to what you say?

Talk in your sleep.

Why is a one-night stand like a newsflash?

It's unexpected, brief and probably a disaster.

Why do men feel more confident with computers than women?

No computer ever laughed at a three-and-a-half-inch floppy.

Why do women get PMS and cellulite?

God made Man first, and he just couldn't help making a few helpful suggestions.

Why are men like clothes stores?

They're most interesting when their clothes are 50% off.

Why do men close their eyes during sex?

They can't stand to see a woman enjoying herself.

12

COMEBACKS AND PUTDOWNS

If my dog looked like you, I'd shave its butt and train it to walk backwards.

Is your name Ex-Lax?

Because you're irritating the shit out of me.

Save your breath—you'll need it to blow up your girlfriend.

I heard you're nobody's fool. Don't worry, maybe someone will adopt you.

Do you always use contraception?

Yes...

Good, so you learned from your parents' mistake.

If you took an IQ test, the results would come back negative.

I didn't know they did condoms in cheese-and-onion flavor! Oh, sorry, you haven't put one on yet...

What's the best position to make an ugly baby?
I don't know.

Well, call your mom, because she certainly does.

Will you miss me?

Why don't you go away and we'll find out.

Sorry, I'm not your type—I'm not inflatable.

A rich man loses his job and tells the wife they'll have to economize. "If you could learn to cook and clean and do the laundry," he says, "we could sack the housekeeper." "And if you could learn to do cunnilingus," she replies, "we could sack the chauffeur."

I bet you're not a virgin.

You're right—because not all men are as ugly as you.

Go out? Yes, we could go to the zoo. They must be wondering where you've been.

Just because you have a prick, doesn't mean you have to act like one.

I bet when you call one of those phone sex lines, the woman on the other end gets an earache.

Have you thought of blind dating? Then you'd only frighten them off with the smell.

You should tell your pants that it's rude to point.

Don't let your mind wander—it's too small to be out on its own.

Is that your birthday suit? You should have asked, I could have ironed it for you.

Go out with you? Sorry, I was about to call Greenpeace and tell them to come and float you off the beach.

You'd better get training—I hear that "ugly" is going to be an Olympic sport.

My dog wouldn't fuck you—not even if you had a pork chop tied around your neck.

You must be a man of rare intelligence—either rare or completely extinct.

Did you know light travels faster than sound?
    That's why you seemed pretty bright until you opened your mouth.

I'd love to fuck your brains out, but it looks like someone else got there first.

If I throw a stick, will you leave?

If I blindfold my dog, I might get it to hump your leg.

You know, you have the body of a god—Buddha.

Tell me everything you know—I have 20 seconds to spare.

I'd like to leave you with one thought. It'd be one more than you've had all evening.

You know, you make me think about sperm.
    Why?
Because you too have a one-in-three million chance, with the help of a woman, of ever becoming a human being.

13

WHAT'S THE DIFFERENCE?

What's the difference between sex and waterskiing?

Nothing. They both start with getting wet between the legs and end up with you on your back.

What's the difference between a man and a cup of coffee?

A cup of coffee can keep you awake all night.

What's the difference between parsley and pubic hair?

A man will push the parsley aside and keep eating.

What's the difference between parsley and pussy?

Nobody eats parsley.

What's the difference between a man and a Rubik cube?

No matter how long you play with a Rubik cube, it'll still be hard.

What's the difference between a penis and chocolate?

Chocolate's still satisfying after it goes soft in your hand.

What's the difference between a clitoris and a golf ball?

Men will spend hours looking for a golf ball.

What's the difference between a man and a battery?

A battery has a positive side.

What's the difference between a sin and a shame?

It's a sin to put it in, but it's a shame to take it out.

What's the difference between a man and a lava lamp?

You only have to turn on a lava lamp once, and it will go up and down indefinitely.

What's the difference between a beer and a man?

The beer comes in a can, not in your mouth.

What's the difference between a dove and a swallow?

One's the bird of peace and the other's the bird of true love.

What's the difference between a condom and a coffin?

A stiff comes in one and goes out in the other.

What's the difference between a turkey and a penis?

It's worth waking up at five in the morning to put a turkey in, because it always lasts long enough to satisfy everyone.

What's the difference between a blood test nurse and a prostitute?

One gets paid to prick lots of fingers and the other gets paid to finger lots of pricks.

What's the difference between a slut and a bitch?

A slut sleeps with everyone. A bitch sleeps with everyone except you.

What's the difference between a bankrupt man and a man who takes Viagra?

They're both hard up, but the bankrupt man can't spend any more.

What's the difference between a man and a Slinky?

Nothing. They're both slightly amusing when they're falling down the stairs, but are otherwise useless.

What's the difference between a lesbian carpenter and a straight carpenter?

One uses tongue and groove, and the other just screws.

What's the difference between medium and rare?

Five inches is medium, ten inches is rare.

What's the difference between a man and a vacation?

Nothing—neither of them is ever long enough.

What's the difference between an infant and an adult?

Infancy isn't nearly as much fun as adultery.

What's the difference between a man and a diaper?

You can change a diaper.

What's the difference between a blonde and a lawyer?

There are some things even a blonde won't do.

What's the difference between monogamy and monotony?

Er—nothing.

What's the difference between a circus and a singles bar?

At a circus the clowns don't talk.

What's the difference between a clitoris and a remote control?

A man can put his hand right on the remote control without looking—every time.

What's the difference between a sweater and a jumper?

With a sweater your sheets are always soaking—with a jumper you don't dare bend over to put them in the washing machine.

What's the difference between a man and a penny?

Every time you toss the penny, you have a 50/50 chance of getting head.

What's the difference between a penis and a bonus check?

It's always fun to blow a man's bonus check.

What's the difference between a cockpit and a box office?

A box office is a place that tries to ensure everyone has a satisfying evening's entertainment. A cockpit is really only concerned with getting up and down.

What's the difference between a gay prince and a booklover?

A booklover uses a bookmark—a gay prince likes his pages bent over.

What's the difference between a man and a lawnmower?

You don't have to suck a lawnmower's exhaust pipe to get it to cut the grass.

What's the difference between a trombonist and a man who plays alto and tenor saxophones?

One's horny and one's bisaxual.

What's the difference between an unlucky mouse and a lucky cock?

Nothing—they both end up inside a satisfied pussy.

What's the difference between circumcision and divorce?

Divorce gets rid of the whole prick.

What's the difference between movie snacks and pictures of naked policemen?

One's popcorn and the other's cop porn!

What's the difference between a child's car seat and a condom?

One stops kids in the back seat from causing accidents, the other stops accidents in the back seat from causing kids.

What's the difference between a curtain and an erection?

A curtain doesn't come down until the performance is finished.

What's the difference between men and concrete?

Both take ages to get hard, but concrete only has to be laid once.

When a man talks dirty to a woman it's sexual harassment.

When a woman talks dirty to a man, it's $3 a minute.

According to a recent survey, men say the first thing that they notice about women is their eyes. Women say the first thing they notice about men is that they're a bunch of liars.

What's the most popular female fantasy?

Having sex with your boyfriend's best friend, a film star, or a stranger on a train.

What's the most popular male fantasy?

Having sex with a woman who isn't fantasizing about somebody else.

What's the difference between a man and a computer?

1. A computer can do more than one job at once.
2. A computer will remember what you told it yesterday.
3. A computer is more impressive the smaller it is.
4. If your computer doesn't have enough hard drive, you can upgrade it.
5. You can still get your work done after you turn a computer on.

6. With a computer, faster is always better.

7. A computer knows the difference between your inbox and your outbox.

8. A computer is more likely to go down on you.

9. A computer can communicate with other computers using words as well as sounds and pictures.

10. A computer can remember important dates like birthdays.

What's the difference between a man and a Christmas tree?

1. The Christmas tree goes up and comes down when you decide it's time.

2. A Christmas tree's balls are nice to look at.

3. No one thinks any worse of you for having an artificial Christmas tree instead of a live one.

4. A Christmas tree doesn't mind when you add an electric device to improve the effect.

5. You can ignore a Christmas tree for 11 months and it'll still be ready next time you want it.

What's the difference between a man and a cat?

1. The only thing a cat leaves all over the house is hair.

2. When a cat sticks its butt in your face, it's not expecting you to lick it.

3. A cat won't fake affection to get what it wants.

4. Cats don't want to watch football.

5. You can stroke a cat twice without it trying to put its tail in your mouth.

6. A cat won't bring you flowers after it's been out all night screwing the neighbor's cat.

7. A hairy back looks good on a cat.

8. Cats can wash themselves.

9. A man only wishes he could lick his own genitals.

10. BUT, if a man brings you a present of a dead animal, it's already been made into a coat.

**What's the difference between a man and
a motorbike?**

1. You can tell how big the exhaust pipe is before
   you start riding it.

2. You can swap motorbikes with your friend to see
   which is the better ride.

3. It's the motorbike that suffers if you don't use
   enough lubrication.

4. A motorbike stays between your legs 'til you've
   had enough fun.

5. You only chain a motorbike up when you've
   finished riding it.

14

MORE SLUTTY BITCH STORIES

"**I** don't know what to get my wife for her birthday," says Bob. "She already has everything, and she earns more than I do, so she can afford to buy anything she wants." "Why don't you give her a voucher saying she can have 60 minutes of great sex, any way she wants?" asks his friend. "Well, I can't think of anything else," says Bob, "so I'll give it a try." The next day, Bob's back in the bar. "I gave her the voucher," he says. "Did she like it?" asks his friend. "Oh yes! She loved it. She kissed me, thanked me for the best present I'd ever given her, and then she ran out of the door shouting, "I'll be back in an hour!"

When John Wayne Bobbit's wife cut off his penis, she drove away with it and threw it out of the car window. Before it landed in the field, it hit the windscreen of another car and bounced off. In the car, a little girl was being driven home by her mother. "Wow!" said the girl. "What was THAT?" "Nothing, honey," replied her embarrassed mother. "Just a fly." "Well," says the girl, "for a little fly, it had a huge penis."

A man goes away on a business trip and, since it's a very swanky hotel, his wife comes to join him for the weekend. They have a nice dinner in the restaurant, a drink in the bar, and then they can't wait to go up to their room. In fact, they can't even wait that long—as soon as they get into the elevator they're all over each other. The man is pulling her panties down and in less than a minute they're at it. Unfortunately, the doors open at the next floor and the housekeeper gets in. "Well, really!" says the housekeeper. "I'm sorry," says the woman, "we just had a couple of drinks and got a bit carried away. I don't normally behave this way." "I'm sure you don't," says the housekeeper, "but this is the fourth time this week I've caught him at it."

A young priest was taking confession in a Catholic school for the first time. "Bless me, Father, for I have sinned," says the first schoolgirl. "I had impure thoughts about my teacher." "Impure thoughts—that's four Hail Marys," says the priest. "Bless me, Father," says the second schoolgirl, "I stole a pencil from the stationery cupboard." "Stealing—that's six Hail Marys," says the priest. But the third schoolgirl says, "Bless me, Father, for I have sinned. I gave my boyfriend a blow job behind the bike sheds." The priest is perplexed—he's never heard this before, and he doesn't know what penance to impose. Slipping out of the confessional, he meets one of the nuns in the chapel. "Quick, Sister Lillian!" he whispers, "What does the Father Colin usually give for a blow job?" "20 bucks." she replies.

* * * *

* Cinderella's going to the ball. "Dress? Check. Crystal carriage? Check. Handsome coachmen? Check. There's just one more thing I need, Fairy Godmother." "What's that, my dear?" "I don't have any contraception." The Fairy Godmother looks around and sees a pumpkin. With a wave of her wand, she turns it into a diaphragm. "Off you go, Cinderella, but remember—you must be home by midnight or your

*

dress will turn back into rags, your carriage will revert to a coal bucket, the coachmen will be mice again and—most importantly—your diaphragm will turn back into a pumpkin!" Cinderella promises to be back by midnight, pops the diaphragm in, and goes off to the ball. At five o'clock in the morning, Cinderella finally rolls in, dressed in rags, carrying a coal bucket full of mice, but smiling happily. "Where have you been?" asks Fairy Godmother. "I told you to be back by midnight!" "I know," sighs Cinderella, "but I met such a nice man." "Prince Charming?" "No, his name was Peter Peter something…"

A man calls his brother, but the brother's wife answers the phone. "Can I speak to George?" "No, I'm afraid George is dead." "What? When did that happen?" "Last night—he died in bed." "How terrible. Did he have any last requests?" "Yes, his last words were, 'Please, put down the gun.'"

Little Red Riding Hood is walking through the forest with her basket when out hops a little rabbit. "Oh, be careful, Little Red Riding Hood," says the rabbit. "The Big Bad Wolf is out hunting. If he catches you, he'll pull up your skirt, pull down your panties and have sex with you!" "Thanks for the warning," replies Little Red Riding Hood, "but I'll be ok." A little further along the path a squirrel pops out of a tree. "Oh, be careful, Little Red Riding Hood," says the squirrel, "The Big Bad Wolf is out hunting. If he catches you, he'll pull up your skirt, pull down your panties and have sex with you!" "Thanks for the warning," replies Little Red Riding Hood, "but really, I'll be ok." After half a mile, the Big Bad Wolf jumps out of the bushes and confronts Little Red Riding Hood. "Now I've caught you," says the Wolf, "I'm going to pull up your skirt, pull

down your panties and have sex with you!" Cool as
anything, Little Red Riding Hood puts her hand into her

basket and pulls out a gun. "I think not," she says,
pointing her gun right at the Big Bad Wolf. "I think
you're going to eat me, just like it says in the book."

A woman is lying in bed with her lover when she hears her husband coming in. "Quick!" she says to her lover, "There's no time to get dressed. Stand in the corner and I'll cover you with talcum powder." In comes the husband and he immediately asks, "Is that a new statue?" "That's right," replies the wife. "The Smiths had one in their bedroom and I liked it so much I got one, too." The husband says nothing else, but gets into bed, leaving the "statue" standing as still as he can in the corner. Around four in the morning, the husband gets up and comes back with a cup of tea and a plate of cookies, which he puts down beside the "statue." "There," he says. "Have a cookie. I was stuck in the Smiths' bedroom for three days, and nobody offered me so much as a drink of water."

An old lady calls the fire department in the middle of the night. "Please come at once—a couple of big hairy bikers are outside, trying to climb up to my bedroom window." "Madam, we're the fire department—you need to call the police." "Why? I thought you were the ones with the ladders!"

A convict escapes from jail, breaks into a house and ties up the young couple that are naked in bed. As they lie there, helpless, the wife says, "Look, we'll do anything you ask. Take what you want—money, food, the car, anything, but don't hurt us." The convict replies, "Well, I've been in jail for 20 years now. I've had nothing to eat but bread and

water; I've had nothing to do but sew mailbags and I haven't set eyes on a woman in all that time." Before the wife can say anything, the husband says, "Take whatever you want. Don't kill us and we'll do anything you want. Anything." "Well then, roll over pretty boy. You remind me of my last cellmate."

A businessman goes to Japan to meet an important client. On his first evening there he meets a beautiful Japanese girl and, in spite of the language barrier, they end up in his hotel room. All night long they have the most amazing sex and every time he feels that he can't go on any more, she starts shouting, "Hitakushi! Hitakushi!" He's not sure what it means, but from the way she's shouting he's guessing that she's having a good time, so he feels like a bit of a stud. The next day, tired but pleased with himself, he meets the client on the golf course, and they talk business over a round of golf. The deal is almost clinched when they reach the 18th hole and the client hits a hole in one. "Hitakushi!" shouts the businessman. The client looks very cross and shouts back at the businessman, "What do you mean, 'wrong hole'?"

A **man turns 40 and decides to treat himself to a facial.** Sure enough, he walks out looking much younger, and feeling very pleased with himself. As he stands in line at the post office he asks the guy at the counter how old he thinks he is. "Maybe 30?" "No! I'm actually 40 today!" And he walks out, very pleased with himself. He goes to the newsstand and asks the newsstand dealer how old he thinks he is. "I don't know—29? 28?" "No! I'm actually 40 today!" He's feeling really good now, and when he gets to the bus

stop he asks an old lady sitting on the bench how old she thinks he is. "To tell you the truth," she replies, "my eyesight isn't what it was, but years ago I worked in a laboratory and we devised a sure-fire scientific method of telling a man's age." "Really?" asks the man, thinking if he can fool a scientific method, he must be looking hot-to-trot. "Yes," replies the old lady. "Shall I try it on you?" So the man agrees and quick as a flash the old lady puts her hand down his pants, inside his underwear, and starts feeling his cock with an expression of intense concentration. After five minutes she pulls her hand out and says, "You are 40 years old—in fact, today is your birthday." "Amazing!" replies the man, "You're right! How did you know that?" "I was behind you in line at the post office."

A couple go skiing, and the man loses his gloves. When they get back to the chalet, he says his hands are frozen. "Well," says the woman, "put them between my thighs and warm them up." The second day, the same thing happens—he can't find his gloves, his hands are frozen, and he puts them between her thighs to warm them up. On the third day he gets up and asks, "Honey, have you seen my earmuffs?"

An old lighthouse keeper lives alone with his wife on a remote rock, until a young assistant is sent to join them. On the first day, the young assistant offers to take the first watch at the top of the lighthouse, so the keeper and his wife can have some time together. "But no sex," he says. "I'm here without a wife or girlfriend, so it wouldn't be fair." The keeper and his wife stroll along the beach hand-in-hand, and the assistant shouts down, "Hey! No sex!" "We're not having sex," calls the keeper. "We're just holding hands." They go and sit outside the keeper's cottage and do a crossword together, but the assistant shouts down, "Hey! I said no sex! It's not fair!" "We're not having sex!" answers the keeper. After lunch, the wife offers to show the assistant around the island, and the keeper goes to the top of the lighthouse. "Well, by golly!" he says to himself. "From up here, it does look exactly like they're having sex!"

A guy sits in a bar wearing jeans, a checkered shirt, cowboy boots and a Stetson hat. A woman comes in, also wearing jeans, a checkered shirt, cowboy boots and a hat and asks, "Say, are you a real cowboy?" "Well," he answers, "my whole life has been spent working with cattle—rounding up

cows, roping calves, branding steers and wrestling bulls. Yep, I guess I must be a real cowboy. But what about you—can I buy you a drink, cowgirl?" "No thanks, cowboy," replies the woman. "You see, I'm a lesbian." "What's that?" "Well, I love women. I wake up in the morning and think about women. I get in the shower and imagine a naked woman there with me. I think about women all day long and the last thing on my mind before I go to sleep is women." "Fair enough," says the cowboy. A few minutes later, another woman comes in and asks him the same question, "Are you a real cowboy?" "Well," he says, "all my life I thought I was a real cowboy, but I just found out I'm a lesbian."

A couple move into an apartment with very thin walls, and they're worried that the neighbors will hear them talking in bed. "I know," says the wife. "When you want sex, put your hand on my breast and squeeze once. If you don't want sex, squeeze it twice." "Ok," says the husband. "If you want sex, put your hand on my penis and pull it once. If you don't want sex, pull it 50 times."

A woman fell off her balcony on the 23rd floor, and as she fell, she prayed, "Oh God, please give me a chance to live!" Suddenly a man leant out from his balcony and caught her in his arms. Before she had a chance to thank him, he asked her, "Do you suck?" "Of course not!" she shouted, thinking this can't be what God intended. So the man let go and she fell again, hurtling towards the ground. Suddenly a second man put out his arms and caught her. "Do you screw?" he asked. "No!" she shouted, wondering what the hell God was playing at, sending all these perverts to catch her. So the man dropped her and she continued to fall. Just as death seemed certain, a third man put out his arms and caught her. Before he could say a word, the woman shouted, "I suck! I screw!" "Slut!" cried the man, and dropped her to her death.

15

SIZE
MATTERS

Why do men give their dicks names?

Because it's always good to be on a first-name basis with the boss.

Mr. Smith hires a gardener who says he's got a huge penis—a foot long relaxed, over a yard erect. When Mrs. Smith hears this she wants to see, so she tells her husband to get the gardener to show it to him while she hides in the shed. The next day, while Mr. Smith and the gardener are cutting the hedge, Mr. Smith asks to see the huge penis. They go to the shed, where Mrs. Smith is hiding, and the gardener gets it out. Impressed, Mr. Smith asks to see it erect, so the gardener rubs it until it grows to be a yard long. The gardener then asks to see Mr. Smith's penis, so he gets his out—it's pretty small. Even when he rubs it, it's only a few inches long. That night, he says to his wife, "I hope you're satisfied. I was

pretty embarrassed when he asked to see mine, too. It
looked so small next to that monster." "You were
embarrassed? I couldn't think of what to say to all my
friends from work who were in the shed with me."

A man loses his penis in an accident and the
doctor offers him an experimental
treatment—they'll take the trunk off a
baby elephant and replace his penis with that. The
operation goes well and he's told not to have sex for six
weeks, until it's completely healed. The six weeks is over

at last and the man is feeling very horny so he plans a romantic night out with his girlfriend at a nice restaurant. When they get there he feels even hornier and his penis starts to swell up. Eventually, he has to unzip his fly and put a napkin over his lap to ease the pressure. The waiter puts a basket of bread on the table and immediately the penis pops out, grabs a bread roll and disappears with it under the napkin. The girlfriend is really impressed. "Perhaps we should skip dessert," she whispers. "Can you do that again?" "Probably," says her boyfriend, "but I don't think I can fit another bread roll up my ass."

Who's the most popular guy in the singles bar?

The one in the corner, licking his eyebrows.

What three words do men hate to hear during sex?

Is it in?

What three words do women hate to hear during sex?

Honey, I'm home!

A man goes to a hypnotherapist to get help for his impotence. While he's hypnotized, the therapist tells him that next time he hears the words "1-2-3" he'll get a huge hard on. When he hears the words "1-2-3-4" it will go down again. The man wakes up and the therapist explains that all he needs to do is say the numbers to control his erection. Very excited, the man can't wait to get into bed with his wife. She's preparing to go straight to sleep as usual when he

slips between the sheets and murmurs, "1-2-3."
Immediately, he starts to swell and gets a huge erection.
Just as he's about to get amorous, his wife rolls over and
asks, "What did you say 1-2-3 for?"

One swallow doesn't make a summer – but it can
make a man's day.

Men are just like children. You give them a lovely toy
for their birthday but they're only happy if you let them
play with the box it comes in.

How do you make your cock look bigger?
  Buy smaller hens.

**"I wanted sex with a fitter, more attractive man, so
I signed my husband up for a slimming group."**
  "Is it working?"
  **"Oh yes—he goes to the meetings every
week—and while he's there his younger, fitter,
more attractive brother comes to my place."**

"Heard about the new Olympic condoms? They come in gold, gold and bronze."

"Why no silver?"

"Do you think a man ever wants to come second?"

Why is sex like snow?

You never know how many inches you're going to get, or how long before it turns to slush.

A woman walks into a drugstore and asks if they sell extra-large condoms.

"Yes, we do—how many do you want?"

"I don't want to buy any—but if anybody else does, can you give them my phone number?"

Little Johnny is at the zoo with his parents, and he sees the male donkey getting rather excited. "What's that, Dad?" he asks, pointing to the large thing he can see underneath the donkey. "Ask your mother, son." So little Johnny trots over to his mother. "What's that, Mom?" "That? That's nothing." Little Johnny still isn't satisfied so he goes back to his dad. "Dad, Dad—what is that? Mom said it was nothing." "Well, she's been spoiled."

"Doctor, I don't seem to be able to get an erection."

"I can't find anything seriously wrong—I think it's the effects of drinking."
"I'll come back when you're sober then."

A man goes to his doctor and says, "D-d-d-d-doctor, y-you've g-g-got to h-h-h-help me! I c-c-c-can't l-live with this st-st-st-stutter any l-l-l-longer!" So the doctor examines him and says, "This is a most unusual case. This stutter is caused by your penis." "M-m-m-my p-p-p-penis?" "Yes, your penis is so long that it's putting strain on the vagus nerve, which is affecting your vocal cords. The only thing I can do is to remove half your penis." Well, the man thinks hard, but eventually he says, "A-a-all r-r-r-right d-d-d-doctor. I c-c-c-can't st-st-stand the sst-st-stuttering. D-d-d-do it!"

A month later, the same man comes back to see the doctor and says, "Look, doctor, you've cured my stutter all right, but my wife says sex just isn't the same with a normal-sized penis. I've thought about it, and I think I'd rather put up with the stutter. Is there any way the operation can be reversed?" And the doctor replies, "Nn-n-no, I'm afraid th-th-th-that's n-n-not p-p-p-possible."

Why do men like big breasts and tight pussies?
Because they've got big mouths and small pricks.

At the fairground, a man sees a sign outside a tent: "Make the horse laugh and win $100." So he goes in. After two minutes the sound of horse laughter comes from the tent, and the man comes out and collects his $100. Next year, the fair is back, but this time the sign outside the tent reads "Make the horse cry and win $100." The same man goes in again, and after two minutes horse sobs are coming from the tent. As the $100 is being counted out, the horse's owner asks the man what his secret is. "Well, last year, I told that horse that my dick was bigger than his. That's why he laughed." "And this year?" "This year, I didn't just tell him, I showed him."

What do you get when you cross a chicken with an onion?

A cock that will bring tears to your eyes.

"My boyfriend can dial my phone number with his tongue."

"That's nothing, mine uses his dictaphone."

Recipe for perfect happiness:

1. A man with a 12-inch penis who can satisfy you all night.
2. A caring man who will do all the housework and wait on you hand and foot.
3. A rich man who showers you with presents.
4. Making sure men 1, 2 and 3 never ever meet.

What's the difference between *A Midsummer Night's Dream* and *Much Ado About Nothing*?

Nine inches is a midsummer night's dream—three inches is much ado about nothing.

Two brothers are having a medical exam, and the doctor comments on the unusual length of their penises. "Yes, sir, we got them from our mother." "Your mother? Surely you inherited them from your father?" "No, sir. You see our mother only has one arm." "One arm? What's that got to do with the length of your penises?" "Well, she had to lift us out of the bath somehow."

Better to have loved and lost a short man than never to have loved a tall.

What do you say to an impotent man?

"No hard feelings."

When God had finished making Adam and Eve he told them he had two gifts left over. "First, the gift of being able to pee standing up…" Before He'd even finished, Adam started shouting, "Oh yes, pee standing up—I'll have that, that'd be great! I'd love that! Please, please, please…" So God, with an indulgent smile, gives Adam the ability to pee standing up. "What's the other one?" asks Eve. "Oh, multiple orgasms…"

ORGASM TYPES

Sex with a rower: oargasm

Sex after falling out of bed: floorgasm

Wet dream: snoregasm

Group sex: fourgasm

Sex for hours and hours: soregasm

Cheap sex: poorgasm

Noisy sex: roargasm

Nymphomaniac sex: Iwantmoregasm

Sex on the beach: shoregasm

Swedish sex: smorgasborgasm

Competitive sex: scoregasm

Sex with a pig: boargasm

Sex on vacation: tourgasm

Sex on the farm: tractorgasm

Sex with a Viking: Thorgasm

What do snails shout during sex?

"Slower! Slower!"

Little Johnny's math teacher asks him to define "average." "It's a kind of bed, Miss," says little Johnny. **"A bed?"** "Yes, I overheard my mom saying she has three orgasms a week on an average."

"Did you come on the bus, Grandma?"

"Yes, dear, but I passed it off as an asthma attack."

A woman walks into the dentist's office, takes off her underwear and sits in the chair with a leg over each arm. "Madam, I think there's some mistake," says the

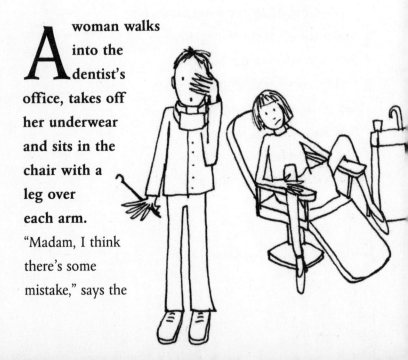

dentist. "The gynecologist's office is on the next floor."
"No mistake," replies the woman. "Yesterday you put in
my husband's new dentures. Today I want you to take
them out."

Why do men prefer to marry virgins?

That way the wife won't know what she's missing.

Bob is having a drink with his friend Bill. "Do you know," says Bill, "there are four kinds of female orgasm: positive, negative, religious and fake." "How do you tell them apart?" asks Bob. "If it's positive, she shouts, 'Oh yes, yes!' Negative is when she shouts, 'Oh no, no!' And the religious orgasm is when she shouts, 'Oh God, oh God!'" "But what does she shout when it's fake?" asks Bob. "She shouts, 'Bob! Bob!'"

Heard about the new stealth condom?

You won't see him coming.

A woman on her deathbed tells her husband to look in the big trunk under the bed. He opens it and finds three eggs and a thousand dollars in cash. "Every time I faked an orgasm with you, I took an egg and I put it in the trunk," says the woman. "Not bad," thinks the man. "Three fakes in all these years of marriage." So he asks the woman, "But what about the thousand dollars?" "Every time I got up to a dozen eggs, I sold them."

How many honest, intelligent, attractive, caring men does it take to truly satisfy a woman?

Both of them.

"You never shout my name when you come!"

"No, I don't want to wake you up."

According to a recent survey, 85% of women masturbate in the shower and the other 15% sing. And do you know what they sing?

Didn't think so.

I was not faking it—I was just practicing so I don't completely forget how to do it.

45% of women celebrate National Orgasm Day every year. The rest just pretend.

An ambulance is called one Sunday morning for a 99-year-old man who has died in bed. To their amazement, he appears to have died while making love to his 98-year-old wife. "We've always done it on Sunday morning," explains his tearful wife, "because at our age, you have to take it slow. We'd listen to the church bells, ding-dong, ding-dong, in-out, in-out—and we'd still be doing it now, if that damned ice-cream van hadn't turned up."

For their 50th wedding anniversary, Bill and Sue go back to the cottage where they spent their honeymoon. As they stroll along a country path, Bill says, "Look, do you remember that tree by the fence?" "I certainly do," blushes Sue. "That's where we had the hottest sex of our honeymoon." Well, they're both still hot for each other, so they look around and, seeing there's nobody in sight, they're soon over by the tree, with Sue leaning against the fence, her skirt hitched up and Bill going at it like a man 50 years younger. In no time, Sue is yelling and thrashing about, and she

doesn't stop until Bill is exhausted and has to sit down on the grass. "I can't have lost my touch," he says proudly. "I don't remember you going that wild 50 years ago." "50 years ago," says Sue, "that fence wasn't electric."

17

KINKS AND QUIRKS

What's the difference between an ice cream and a masochist?

An ice cream is often licked but never beaten...

Two newlyweds arrive at their honeymoon hotel, and ask for a double room. "Since it's your honeymoon," says the receptionist, "wouldn't you like the bridal suite?" "No, it's all right," says the bridegroom. "I'll just hold on to her ears until she gets the hang of it."

What's black and white and red-hot?

A nun with pierced nipples.

Why didn't the flasher retire early?

He decided he could stick it out for another year.

What's the difference between sexy and kinky?

Sexy is using a feather—kinky is when it's still attached to the chicken.

Why is rimming like drinking whiskey?

They both leave you shitfaced.

What do you call a man who's gagged and tied to the bed?

Trustworthy.

How do you spot really sexy shoes?

You can get them off with one finger.

What's the difference between a masochist and a mosquito?

If you hit a mosquito, it'll stop eating you.

What's the word for a man who's watching a woman undress?

Grateful.

Why do sadists take so long to get to the point?

Because they're always beating around the bush.

An Englishman, an Irishman and a Scotsman are being interviewed for the priesthood and they're told they have to pass a celibacy test to see if they're capable of controlling their carnal urges. They stand naked in a room and a small bell is tied to each of their pricks to reveal the slightest arousal. A beautiful woman is then brought in and she starts to perform a striptease. *Ting-a-ling!* The Irishman's bell rings as his prick stirs uncontrollably. Then the naked woman approaches the Scotsman and starts to blow on his neck. *Ting-a-ling!* The Scotsman's bell rings. Now the two have huge erections, but the Englishman is not aroused at all. The woman runs her hands all over his naked body, but nothing—his bell remains silent. At last the priest says, "Enough! You have proved yourself worthy of the priesthood. As for you other two, your punishment shall be a severe paddling." *Ting-a-ling!* goes the Englishman's bell.

A woman stopped to admire her neighbor's tomatoes. "How do you get them so red?" she asks. "I must admit," he says, "I'm a bit of an exhibitionist and I like to flash in my garden. I think the tomatoes blush every time I do it, that's why they're so red." "Thank you, I might try that myself," she says. A few weeks later the same man sees the woman digging her own garden, but her tomatoes are still green. "So you didn't try my technique?" he asks her. "Oh yes," she says. "My tomatoes stayed the same—but my cucumbers are huge."

What's the difference between a pickpocket and a voyeur?

A pickpocket snatches your watch and a voyeur watches your snatch.

What do you call a thick book about voyeurism?

A peeping tome.

Heard about the transvestite who lost the high-heel-wearing contest?

He suffered the agony of defeat.

Ever thought of dating a necrophiliac?

Over my dead body!

What's the difference between a man and a vibrator?

They haven't made a vibrator that can mow the lawn.

An old rancher marries a young wife, hoping she can help with the hard work, but soon it's clear that they need more help, so they hire a strapping young cowboy to help around the place. After a month the rancher's wife says to the rancher, "Hank's worked so hard, I think he deserves a night off. Let's tell him he can ride into town, and I'll wait up to let him in when he gets back." The rancher agrees, and Hank rides into town.

When he gets back, the rancher's wife is sitting in the kitchen waiting for him. "Come in, Hank," she says. "Now, I want you to take off my shoes." "Yes, Ma'am," says Hank, and he takes off her little button boots. "Very good, Hank. Now take off my skirt." So Hank slips off her skirt. "Now Hank, take off my stockings and my corset." So Hank takes off her stockings and her corset. "And finally, Hank, I want you to take off my panties." So Hank takes off her panties. "Very good, Hank. Now, if I ever catch you wearing my clothes to town again, you're fired."

A nun gets into a taxi. As he drives her along, the taxi driver says he has a confession to make—he's always had a sexual thing about nuns. As he's just been told he has a terminal illness it would mean a lot to him if he could have sex with a nun just once before he dies. "Well, my son," says the nun, "in view of your tragic circumstances, it is my duty to do what I can for you. I will have sex with you on one condition—obviously I can't get pregnant, so I'll have to take it up the tradesman's entrance." The taxi driver gets in the back, lifts up the nun's habit and screws her soundly.

Afterwards, the taxi driver starts to cry. "I feel so guilty," he says. "I lied to you to get you to have sex with me. I don't really have a terminal illness at all." "That's all right," says the nun. "I lied to you as well—my name's Kevin and I'm on my way to a costume party."

A **punk rocker gets on a bus: he's pierced and tattooed, with multicolored hair in a big Mohawk.** He sees an old man staring and asks, "What's the matter old boy—didn't you ever do anything wild in your life?" "Yes," says the old man. "I had sex with a parrot once, and I was just wondering if you were my son."

Why couldn't they get funding for a porn film about flagellation, bestiality and necrophilia?

Everyone said they were beating a dead horse.

What's a shepherd's favorite love song?

"I only have eyes for ewe!"

Pervert's Dictionary

Biodegradable: likes to be humiliated by lovers of either sex

Combination: to achieve orgasm in order of nationality

Deferred: shaved pubic hair

Erectile: to be turned on by flooring

Gaggle: sound made by someone trying to laugh while wearing a gag

Hamstring: what Hollywood stars do with a small rodent

Hermitage: when the woman wears gloves

Hertz: sadistic sex

Liposuction: a blow job

Megahertz: really sadistic sex

Multitude: oral sex with lots of partners

Mystical: a dominatrix with a feather duster

Negligent: a man who likes to wear frilly nightwear

Permitted: wearing gloves while dressed as Catwoman
Rectitude: rimming
Referred: pubic hair grown back
Stalemate: wife-swapping
Tourist liaison: a pair of handcuffs

Why did the sadist steal the batteries for the vibrator?

Because he liked to take charge.

Why did the pervert like the chicken?

He thought it was poultry in motion.

My husband bought a waterbed but then we started to drift apart.

I wanted to be a streaker but I wasn't suited for it.

A man goes to a brothel and asks for the kinkiest girl they have. "I'm sorry, sir, all our girls are busy, but if you like you can have the pig." He thinks it's pretty kinky, so he has sex with the pig. Next week he's back, asking for the kinkiest girl they have. "I'm sorry, sir, all our girls are busy." "Well, can I have the pig again?" "No, sorry, sir, no pig, but if you like you can go into the room at the end and watch." So he goes into the room at the end and there are a dozen guys all masturbating, watching through a pane of glass while a woman licks melted chocolate off a man who is tied to the bed. "Wow!" he says, "That's pretty hot!" "You think this is good," says one of the other guys, "there was some pervert in there last week, having sex with a pig."

It's ok to use food in sex, but be safe—always use a condiment.

Some perverts like to watch a woman wrestle, but most men prefer to see her box.

What do you get if you cross a pervert and a hamster?

Letters from animal rights campaigners.

A man walks into the bedroom naked but entirely wrapped in plastic and says to his wife, "Tell me the truth, do you think I'm a pervert?" "I don't know about pervert," replies his wife, **"but I can clearly see you're nuts."**

Some people like bondage, but it's knot for everyone.

Why does a man with a pierced cock make the best husband?

He's experienced pain and he knows how to buy jewelry.

A woman passes a pet shop and sees a sign reading, "Clitoris-licking Frog." So she goes in and says, "I've come for the clitoris-licking frog." The assistant answers, "Oui, Madame?"

What kind of candy do perverts eat?

S&M&Ms.

What does a transvestite do at Christmas?

Eat, drink and be Mary.

Why is virgin wool so expensive?

Because you can only get it from ugly sheep.

How do you know when you're at a sadist's wedding?

They use real pain for the toasts instead of champagne.

How many perverts does it take to put in a light bulb?

Only one, but you have to go to the emergency room to get it taken out.

A woman goes into a sex shop and asks to see the dildos. The assistant shows her a black one, but she says it's too small. He shows her a pink one, but that's still too small. Then he shows her a chrome one, but she says none of them will do. Finally, she points to the big tartan one on the top shelf, and says she'll have that one. A few minutes later the manager gets back from lunch and asks how it's going. "Great—I sold one black dildo, two pink dildos, three chrome dildos—and your thermos."

Other Books from Ulysses Press

MAN WALKS INTO A BAR
Stephen Arnott &Mike Haskins, $14.95
Everyone loves a good joke. Even more so, everyone wants to be the
person telling it and sending everybody in the room into hysterics. Man
Walks into a Bar is packed full of quick and easy jokes that are as simple to
remember and repeat as they are funny. After only a few pages, readers will
be telling these side-splitting jokes to friends, family and coworkers.

THE ULTIMATE DIRTY JOKE BOOK
Mike Oxbent & Harry P. Ness, $9.95
These are the jokes that no one dares to tell in polite company – this book
holds back nothing and guarantees outrageous laughs.

DIRTY ITALIAN: EVERYDAY SLANG FROM "WHAT'S UP?" TO "F*%# OFF!"
Gabrielle Euvino, $10.00
Nobody speaks in strictly formal address anymore. Certainly not in Italy,
where the common expression shouted on the streets is far from textbook
Italian. This all-new, totally-up-to-date book fills in the gap between how
people really talk in Italy and what Italian language students are taught.

DIRTY JAPANESE: EVERYDAY SLANG FROM "WHAT'S UP?"
TO "F*%# OFF!"
Matt Fargo, $10.00
Even in traditionally minded Japan, slang from its edgy pop culture
constantly enter into common usage. This book fills in the gap between how
people really talk in Japan and what Japanese language students are taught.

To order these books call 800-377-2542 or 510-601-8301, fax 510-601-
8307, e-mail ulysses@ulyssespress.com, or write to Ulysses Press, P.O. Box
3440, Berkeley, CA 94703. All retail orders are shipped free of charge.
California residents must include sales tax. Allow two to three weeks for
delivery.